MOON BASE AND BEYOND

THE LUNAR GATEWAY TO DEEP SPACE

ALICIA Z. KLEPEIS

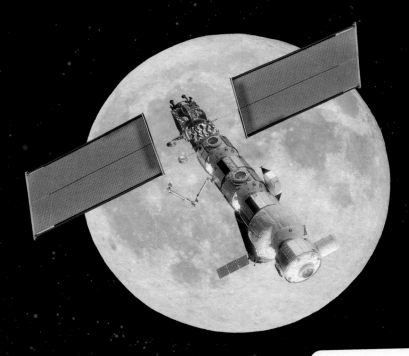

CONTENT CONSULTANT
SARAH RUIZ
Aerospace Engineer

D1451258

CAPSTONE PRESS
a capstone imprint

Edge Books are published by Capstone Press,
1710 Roe Crest Drive, North Mankato, Minnesota 56003
www.capstonepub.com

Library of Congress Cataloging-in-Publication Data
Names: Klepeis, Alicia, 1971– author.
Title: Moon base and beyond : the lunar gateway to deep space / by Alicia Z. Klepeis.
Description: North Mankato, MN: Capstone Press, [2019] | Series: Edge books.
Future space | "Edge Books are published by Capstone Press." | Audience: Age 9. |
Audience: Grades 4 to 6. | Includes bibliographical references and index.
Identifiers: LCCN 2019003343|
ISBN 9781543572759 (ebook pdf) | ISBN 9781543572674 (library binding)
ISBN 9781543575156 (pbk.)
Subjects: LCSH: Lunar bases—Juvenile literature. | Space stations—Juvenile literature. |
Space flight to the moon—Juvenile literature. | Moon—Exploration—Juvenile literature. |
Outer space—Exploration—Juvenile literature.
Classification: LCC TL799.M6 K54 2019 | DDC 629.44/2—dc23
LC record available at https://lccn.loc.gov/2019003343

Editorial Credits
Mandy Robbins, editor; Laura Mitchell, designer; Jo Miller, media researcher;
Katy LaVigne, production specialist

Image Credits
NASA, Cover (spacecraft), 1 (spacecraft), 7, 9, 11, 13, 15, 16–17, 19, 21, 26; Science Source: Chris
Butler, 23, ESA/Foster + Partners, 25, Victor Habbick Visions, 29; Shutterstock: Belish, Cover
(moon), 1 (moon), Romolo Tavani, 5

Design Elements
Capstone; Shutterstock: Audrius Birbilas e

All internet sites appearing in back matter were available and accurate when this book was sent to press.

Printed and bound in the United States of America.
PA70

TABLE OF CONTENTS

CHAPTER ONE

MOON MISSIONS PAST AND PRESENT

Imagine living in space. You're **orbiting** the moon aboard a new space station. The air smells of a weird mix of garbage and cleaning supplies. Fans and pumps hum as they constantly work to keep the air around you clean. LED lights make it feel like daytime. Through the window, you see clouds swirling over the blue globe of Earth.

Your day begins in the laboratory, doing science experiments. Later, your spacecraft travels closer to the moon. You can clearly see its craters and peaks. Conditions are great for a trip to the surface. Dressed in your spacesuit, you collect rock and dust samples to bring back to the station. You hope to learn more about the history of the moon and the Earth from these samples.

Imagine living on the moon and seeing Earth in the sky as you see the moon now.

This scenario might seem far off in the future. But it's not. Astronauts could be living and researching in **lunar** orbit and on the surface of the moon by the mid-2020s.

SPACE FACT:

We always see the same side of the moon from Earth. That's because it spins around at the same rate that it orbits Earth.

lunar—having to do with a moon

orbit—to travel around an object in space; an orbit is also the path an object follows while circling an object in space

EARLY MOON EXPLORATION

The moon has fascinated people for thousands of years. But humans didn't have the technology to get there until the 1950s. In 1959, the former Soviet Union successfully landed a small spacecraft called Luna 2 on the moon. Between 1968 and 1972, the United States' National Aeronautics and Space Administration (NASA) sent nine manned missions to the moon. Japan, China, and India have sent unmanned moon missions, too.

Today the United States has a new plan called Space Policy Directive 1. It puts exploring the moon at the top of NASA's "to-do" list for the first time in nearly 50 years. But the way astronauts explore the moon will change. The Apollo 11 crew spent less than 22 hours there in 1969. Future astronauts might spend six weeks at a time circling the moon and exploring its surface. Eventually, the moon could be a jumping off point for places farther out in deep space, to Mars and beyond!

SPACE FACT:

Technology has come a long way since the first moon missions. A smartphone has more computing power than NASA had during the 1960s and early 1970s.

Astronauts Buzz Aldrin (pictured) and Neil Armstrong became the first people to set foot on the moon in 1969.

CHAPTER TWO

GATEWAY

NASA is leading an international effort to build the Lunar Orbital Platform-Gateway. This mini space station, nicknamed "Gateway," will orbit the moon. Astronaut crews will live and work there. They will test new technologies for exploring in deep space. Crews will stay at the Gateway for up to six weeks. Even when no one is living there, scientific tools on the inside and outside of Gateway will continue to gather data.

SPACE FACT:

The Japanese, Canadian, and European space agencies plan to use Gateway for a robotic mission to the moon in the 2020s.

Astronauts at Gateway will also make judgments about possible living arrangements for future missions. Perhaps they will discover that smaller habitats are too difficult for long-term missions. They might find better ways to use the small spaces they have. Astronauts living on the International Space Station (ISS) today have much more space than those on Gateway will. The inside of the ISS is about the size of a five-bedroom house. But Gateway will be more like living in a camper.

🚀	GATEWAY	ISS
WEIGHT	75 TONS	450 TONS
DISTANCE FROM EARTH	MORE THAN 200,000 MILES (321,869 KM)	250 MILES (402 KM)
HABITABLE MODULES*	2-3	15
NUMBER OF RESIDENTS	4	6
LENGTH OF STAY	UP TO 6 WEEKS	UP TO 6 MONTHS (TYPICALLY)

POWER AND PROPULSION UNIT

GATEWAY'S DESIGN

Engineers have designed Gateway to have six or seven units called **modules**. They will fit together to form the station. Each module will have a specific purpose. There will likely be two modules to house the astronauts. The astronauts will live and do research there. Another module will provide solar electric power. That electricity will power the station's lights, computers, fans, and more.

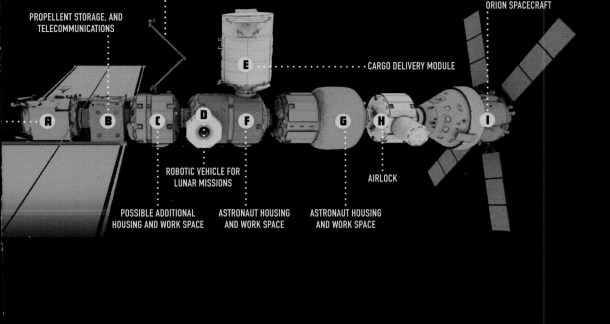

ORION SPACECRAFT

PROPELLENT STORAGE, AND
TELECOMMUNICATIONS

E .... • CARGO DELIVERY MODULE

A   B   C   D   F   G   H   I

ROBOTIC VEHICLE FOR
LUNAR MISSIONS

AIRLOCK

POSSIBLE ADDITIONAL
HOUSING AND WORK SPACE

ASTRONAUT HOUSING
AND WORK SPACE

ASTRONAUT HOUSING
AND WORK SPACE

One module will serve as a docking port. This
is a bit like a garage where spacecraft coming to
Gateway can both "park" and depart from. It will also
serve as an **airlock** for astronauts going on **space
walks**. There will also be modules for power
storage and communication, as well as for intake of
cargo deliveries. A final module called the Orion
Spacecraft could carry the crew out into deep space.

airlock—the enclosure between two airtight doors to permit
passage from one space to the other

module—a separate section that can be linked to other parts

space walk—a period of time during which an astronaut leaves
the spacecraft to move around in space

BUILDING GATEWAY

So how and where will Gateway be built? The plan is for unmanned rockets to send the various parts for Gateway into space. The lunar modules will then be assembled while in orbit.

The first Gateway hardware is scheduled to ship from Earth in 2022. The power and **propulsion** element (PPE) will be shipped from Earth first. The PPE will maintain Gateway's position and move it between different locations. The PPE will also provide Gateway's communications. Several other parts will be launched after the PPE, followed by the airlock. Later on, another module will allow cargo missions to bring supplies to the Gateway.

How An Airlock Works

Humans can't breathe in space. Because of this, space stations must have something called an airlock. It is a small room between outer space and the space station. It keeps the air from leaking out of the space station. To go on a space walk, an astronaut dressed in a spacesuit would step into the airlock. The outside door would be closed. Once inside, the astronaut would close the inside door. All of the air would then be pumped out of the airlock. Then the astronaut would open the outside door and head into space.

Special ropes called tethers connect astronauts to the spacecraft so they don't float away.

Building Gateway will likely be an international effort. Russia may be building the airlock module. Japan may provide a unit to help with communications and propulsion. Canada might construct a robotic arm for outdoor work at Gateway. NASA will provide one housing module. One of its international partners will provide the other. Scientists from around the world could benefit from Gateway. NASA officials think the Gateway could be ready to house astronauts by the mid-2020s.

propulsion—the thrust or power that makes an aircraft or spacecraft move forward

CHAPTER THREE

MOON VEHICLES AND LANDING

Space agencies and private companies are currently working on developing new space vehicles. One spacecraft is called Orion. Astronauts will travel to and from Gateway in Orion. This exploration vehicle is built for deep space. Orion could travel to Mars or even an asteroid.

Orion needs a boost to be lifted into orbit. So it will launch on top of a giant rocket called the Space Launch System (SLS). It will be able to launch Orion while also carrying heavy cargo, such as Gateway modules and landers. It will carry more **cargo** to lunar orbit than any previous vehicles.

SPACE FACT:

Shipping items from Earth into space can cost more than $25,000 per pound!

The Launch Abort System (LAS) is an important part of Orion. In case of an emergency during launch, the LAS would propel the crew module a safe distance away from the rocket. A parachute system would allow the module to land safely back on the ground. The LAS breaks away once Orion reaches orbit.

cargo—the goods carried by a vehicle

NASA's Lunar Electric Rover

LANDING ON THE MOON

When the Apollo spacecraft traveled to the moon, it flew in a circular path about 60 miles (97 kilometers) from the moon's surface. It was only able to land near the moon's **equator**. That won't be the case with Gateway.

Gateway's orbit will vary in its distance to the moon's surface. The astronauts aboard Gateway will be able to choose where they want to land on the moon's surface. This will give them far more opportunities to learn about different parts of the moon. The parts can include the moon's poles, impact craters, and **lava tubes**.

Once Gateway crew members choose a location, they will take a special landing vehicle down to the surface. In the past, different rovers or lunar vehicles explored the moon's surface and were then left behind. They are all still on the moon! Today space agencies are working to develop reusable vehicles to explore on future missions.

SPACE FACT:

Scientists have tested the incredible 10-foot- (3-meter-) tall Lunar Electric Rover in the Arizona desert. Its pressurized cabin has fold-down beds, a sink, a toilet, and even a collapsible exercise bike!

equator—an imaginary line around the middle of a planet or body in space

lava tube—a natural tunnel formed by a lava flow

CHAPTER FOUR

SCIENCE IN SPACE

Humans have already been to the moon. They've collected rocks from its surface. **Probes** have provided scientists with tons of information. But they have only scratched the surface. There's still so much to learn about the moon and deep space beyond.

Instruments mounted on the outside of Gateway will help make observations of Earth, the moon, and the solar system. Scientists will also operate robots remotely to explore the moon's surface more closely. Unlike humans, robots could explore in the vacuum of space without time limits. They could also gather samples on the moon's surface and bring them to Gateway for astronauts to study.

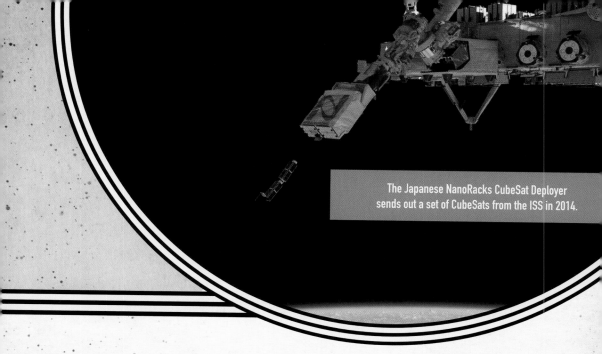

The Japanese NanoRacks CubeSat Deployer sends out a set of CubeSats from the ISS in 2014.

Astronauts will send CubeSats from Gateway as well. A CubeSat is a tiny cube-shaped research spacecraft. It's only about 4 inches (10 centimeters) long and weighs 3 pounds (1.4 kilograms). These tiny **satellites** could investigate asteroids or measure **radiation**. They may also seek out future landing sites at different locations in space.

SPACE FACT:

Two CubeSats, nicknamed "Wall-E" and "Eva," were the first to travel to another planet. They headed to Mars in May 2018. They completed their mission in November 2018.

probe—a small vehicle used to explore objects in outer space

radiation—dangerous rays of energy given off by certain elements

satellite—an object that moves around a cosmic body; a spacecraft used to send signals and information from one place to another

HUMANS IN DEEP SPACE

One goal of going back to the moon is to learn more about how deep space affects the human body. ISS crew members have made many discoveries through experiments using their own bodies. For example, they have found it is possible to reduce the bone and muscle loss in space with certain exercises.

You may wonder, if astronauts can learn about their bodies in space on the ISS, why travel farther from Earth? Deep space may affect the human body in different ways from low-Earth orbit. Scientists need to know more about the risks of radiation exposure in deep space before sending astronauts to Mars and beyond.

Crews aboard the Gateway will also have to hone their survival skills in deep space. They'll have to train for emergency situations in which they'd be too far to get help from Earth. Machinery might break. A crew member might have a serious health crisis. Astronauts need to plan how to solve possible problems before they occur millions of miles from home.

Astronauts on the ISS exercise about two hours a day to keep muscles and bones from getting weak.

CHAPTER FIVE

A LUNAR COLONY

People have dreamed of living on the moon for hundreds of years. But there are many challenges to living there. There is no oxygen to breathe. The temperature swings from minus 387 degrees Fahrenheit (minus 233 degrees Celsius) at night to 253°F (123°C) during the day. There is also no **atmosphere** to protect humans from the Sun's dangerous radiation.

SPACE FACT:

New research suggests that concrete made of moon soil and rocks could be stronger than concrete made on Earth.

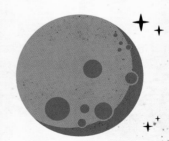

A moon habitat would have to be airtight. It would have to provide a steady stream of breathable air for its residents without leaking. It would also need to be temperature controlled. A moon habitat must be very strong and sturdy. It would have to withstand space rocks that often rain down onto the moon's surface. It would need a water recycling system, because water is limited there. A system to generate power would also be needed. A place would be needed for residents to store and prepare food. It may even have a place for residents to grow food. The technology for such a plan is just starting to develop.

atmosphere—the layer of gases that surrounds some planets, dwarf planets, and moons

BUILDING A MOON BASE

Building a moon base would be an enormous undertaking. Some experts think a great location might be in the deep craters near the moon's poles. These super cold locations likely contain frozen water. Astronauts could use this resource.

According to NASA, before construction for a moon base begins, robots might build the landing site for a moon outpost. Two robots could stabilize the moon's loose soil. They'd also build walls around the launch pads. Using robots would be safer and less expensive than having people do this kind of construction.

Water On The Moon

For many years, people thought the moon was completely dry. But in 2009, a satellite called the Lunar Crater Observation and Sensing Satellite (LCROSS) proved them wrong. The LCROSS was purposely crashed into a crater near the moon's south pole. The crash kicked up more than 26 gallons (98.5 liters) of water! This could provide a vital lifeline to those visiting or living on the moon.

The European Space Agency is researching the possibility of building
a moon base like the one pictured using lunar soil in a 3-D printer.

What might the construction process look like?
First, a space rocket would transport the base
of the moon colony. It would be folded up into a
tube-shaped module. Next, an inflatable dome
would stretch from one end of the module to the
other. This would provide a sturdy support structure
for construction. Then a robot-operated 3-D printer
would make building blocks out of the moon's own
dust, soil, and rock. These would go over the dome
and provide a protective shell for the lunar base.

Astronaut Don Petit floats among several bags of trash before they are disposed from the ISS.

To PMA2   DECK

SPACE FACT:

Past lunar missions have left some interesting waste on the moon. It includes three lunar rovers, several cameras, a family photo, and nearly 100 packets of human waste.

HUMANS IN DEEP SPACE

Whether on Earth or in space, people must eat and dispose of their trash. But these tasks are more difficult and expensive in deep space. Humans must find creative options. NASA scientists think it may be possible for astronauts to grow plants while living on the moon.

In the future, "space farms" may provide much of the food needed by astronauts. These indoor greenhouses will have special lamps to help plants thrive in the controlled environment of a spacecraft. Space gardens could also recycle waste and make more oxygen. For long trips into space, freshly grown produce would have more nutrients than food brought from Earth months earlier.

Managing trash in deep space will be a real challenge. ISS trash is loaded onto empty cargo ships and burned up during the trip back down through Earth's atmosphere. But there won't be as many resupply missions to Gateway as there are to the ISS. Companies are developing ways of squeezing trash to make it easier to store. NASA is also exploring the use of **biodegradable** packaging material.

biodegradable—a substance or object that breaks down naturally in the environment

THE FUTURE OF
SPACE EXPLORATION

Over the next 10 years, astronauts will likely learn a great deal about living and researching in deep space from the area near the moon. But in the near future, Gateway may serve as a jumping off point for missions to Mars and beyond.

It's an exciting time for space exploration and scientific discoveries. We could discover more about the human body in deep space, about the moon, and about what lies beyond. But it will take an international effort to tackle the challenges of being farther away from the comforts of Earth.

Maybe you will be an astronaut or a space tourist in the future. You might drop off supplies at Gateway for crew members on their way to an asteroid. Or maybe you'll build a space farm that will feed the hungry residents of a moon colony. In the not-too-distant future, maybe you'll help mine asteroids or leave your boot prints on Mars' red soil!

It may not be long before humans have a thriving colony on the moon!

GLOSSARY

airlock (AIR-lok)—the enclosure between two airtight doors to permit passage from one space to the other

atmosphere (AT-muh-sfeer)—the layer of gases that surrounds some planets, dwarf planets, and moons

biodegradable (by-oh-dee-GRAY-duh-buhl)—a substance or object that breaks down naturally in the environment

cargo (KAR-goh)—goods transported in a vehicle, ship, or aircraft

equator (i-KWAY-tuhr)—an imaginary line around the middle of a planet or body in space

lava tube (LAHV-uh TOOB)—a natural tunnel formed by a lava flow

lunar (LOO-nuhr)—having to do with a moon

module (MAW-juhl)—a separate section that can be linked to other parts

orbit (OR-bit)—to travel around an object in space; an orbit is also the path an object follows while circling an object in space

probe (PROBE)—a small vehicle used to explore objects in outer space

propulsion (pruh-PUHL-shun)—the thrust or power that makes an airplane or rocket move forward

radiation (ray-dee-AY-shuhn)—dangerous rays of energy given off by certain elements

satellite (SAT-uh-lite)—an object that moves around a planet or other cosmic body; often a spacecraft used to send signals and information from one place to another

space walk (SPAYS WAK)—a period of time during which an astronaut leaves the spacecraft to move around in space

READ MORE

Loh-Hagan, Virginia. *Apollo 13: Mission To The Moon*. True Survival. Ann Arbor, MI: 45th Parallel Press/Cherry Lake Publishing, 2018.

Mahoney, Emily. *What Is On The Far Side Of The Moon?* Space Mysteries. New York: Gareth Stevens Publishing, 2019.

Scott, Elaine. *Our Moon: New Discoveries About Earth's Closest Companion*. Boston: Clarion Books, 2015.

INTERNET SITES

Build a Moon Habitat!
https://spaceplace.nasa.gov/moon-habitat/en/

Moon Exploration
https://www.esa.int/esaKIDSen/SEMXR6WJD1E_OurUniverse_0.html

Moon Exploration
https://www.nationalgeographic.com/science/space/space-exploration/moon-exploration/

Moon Mission
https://www.msn.com/en-us/kids/science-tech/moon-mission/ar-BBN1gVb

INDEX